DINOSAUR FACT DIG

ALLOSAURUS
AND ITS RELATIVES
THE NEED-TO-KNOW FACTS

BY
MEGAN
COOLEY PETERSON

Consultant: Mathew J. Wedel, PhD
Associate Professor
Western University of Health Services

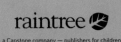

raintree

a Capstone company — publishers for children

Raintree is an imprint of Capstone Global Library Limited, a company incorporated in England and Wales having its registered office at 264 Banbury Road, Oxford, OX2 7DY – Registered company number: 6695582

www.raintree.co.uk
myorders@raintree.co.uk

EDITORIAL CREDITS
Michelle Hasselius, editor; Kazuko Collins, designer; Wanda Winch, media researcher; Gene Bentdahl, production specialist

ISBN 978 1 474 7 2825 6
20 19 18 17 16
10 9 8 7 6 5 4 3 2 1

British Library Cataloguing in Publication Data
A full catalogue record for this book is available from the British Library.

ACKNOWLEDGEMENTS
All images by Jon Hughes except: MapArt (maps), Shutterstock: Elena Elisseeva, green gingko leaf, Jiang Hongyan, yellow gingko leaf, Taigi, paper background

We would like to thank Dr Mathew J. Wedel for his invaluable help in the preparation of this book.

Every effort has been made to contact copyright holders of material reproduced in this book. Any omissions will be rectified in subsequent printings if notice is given to the publisher.

All the internet addresses (URLs) given in this book were valid at the time of going to press. However, due to the dynamic nature of the internet, some addresses may have changed, or sites may have changed or ceased to exist since publication. While the author and publisher regret any inconvenience this may cause readers, no responsibility for any such changes can be accepted by either the author or the publisher.

Printed and bound in China.

CONTENTS

Allosaurus was a fearsome, meat-eating dinosaur. Using its sawlike teeth and sharp claws, it attacked other dinosaurs.

Some of the biggest meat-eating dinosaurs belonged to the Allosaurus family. Carcharodontosaurus and Giganotosaurus may have been even bigger than Tyrannosaurus rex! Read on to learn more about Allosaurus and its relatives.

ACROCANTHOSAURUS

PRONOUNCED: ACK-roh-KAN-thuh-SAWR-us

NAME MEANING: high-spined lizard

TIME PERIOD LIVED: Early Cretaceous Period

LENGTH: 11 metres (35 feet)

WEIGHT: 4.4 metric tons (4.9 tons)

TYPE OF EATER: carnivore

PHYSICAL FEATURES: sail down its back; sharp claws and teeth; strong legs

ACROCANTHOSAURUS was as long as Tyrannosaurus rex but weighed less.

Only four **ACROCANTHOSAURUS** skeletons have been found so far.

Acrocanthosaurus lived in the forests and swamps of what is now the USA, in Oklahoma, Texas and Utah.

N

W — E

S

■ where this dinosaur lived

ACROCANTHOSAURUS' eyes faced to the side. It cocked its head to one side to see prey.

ALLOSAURUS

PRONOUNCED: AL-oh-SAWR-us

NAME MEANING: strange reptile

TIME PERIOD LIVED: Late Jurassic Period

LENGTH: 8.5 metres (28 feet)

WEIGHT: 2.7 metric tons (3 tons)

TYPE OF EATER: carnivore

PHYSICAL FEATURES: long tail; curved claws; travelled on two legs; jagged teeth

ALLOSAURUS was the most common dinosaur in North America during the Late Jurassic Period.

ALLOSAURUS may have hunted in packs. A pack could kill very large prey.

Allosaurus lived on plains in
what is now North America.

N
W E
S

where this
dinosaur
lived

At the Cleveland-Lloyd Quarry in Utah, USA,
scientists have found baby **ALLOSAURUS**
fossils that are the size of dogs.

AUCASAURUS

PRONOUNCED: AW-ka-SAWR-us

NAME MEANING: Auca lizard; named after Auca Mahuevo, the site where it was discovered

TIME PERIOD LIVED: Late Cretaceous Period

LENGTH: 5.5 metres (18 feet)

WEIGHT: 680 kilograms (1,500 pounds)

TYPE OF EATER: carnivore

PHYSICAL FEATURES: sawlike teeth; strong back legs and tail

AUCASAURUS was a fast runner. It could chase prey at high speeds.

AUCASAURUS is one of the best-known meat-eaters. All of its bones have been found except for the ones at the end of its tail.

Aucasaurus lived on the plains of what is now Argentina.

N

W ← → E

S

where this dinosaur lived

AUCASAURUS had very short arms. Its hands were not able to reach each other.

BARYONYX

PRONOUNCED: BEAR-ee-ON-icks

NAME MEANING: heavy claw

TIME PERIOD LIVED: Early Cretaceous Period

LENGTH: 10 metres (32.8 feet)

WEIGHT: 1.2 metric tons (1.3 tons)

TYPE OF EATER: carnivore

PHYSICAL FEATURES: long crocodile-like jaw and teeth; big claw on each hand

In 1983 fossil hunter William Walker found the first **BARYONYX** bone. He unearthed a 25-centimetre (10-inch) long claw.

Baryonyx lived near the waters of what are now England and Spain.

Partially digested fish bones, scales and the bones of a baby Iguanodon were found inside a **BARYONYX**.

N
W E
S

where this dinosaur lived

Scientists nicknamed the first **BARYONYX** specimen "Claws".

CARCHARODONTOSAURUS

PRONOUNCED: car-CARE-oh-DON-toh-SAWR-us

NAME MEANING: shark-tooth lizard

TIME PERIOD LIVED: Late Cretaceous Period

LENGTH: 12 metres (40 feet)

WEIGHT: 6 metric tons (6.6 tons)

TYPE OF EATER: carnivore

PHYSICAL FEATURES: large jaw to swallow its prey whole; sharp teeth

CARCHARODONTOSAURUS had a larger skull than Tyrannosaurus rex, but its brain was smaller.

Carcharodontosaurus lived in the deserts and swamps of what are now Algeria, Egypt, Morocco and Niger.

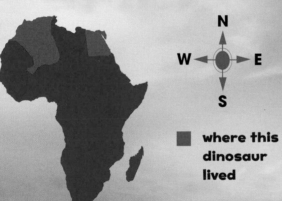

N
W——E
S

■ where this dinosaur lived

CARCHARODONTOSAURUS had knifelike teeth about 20 centimetres (8 inches) long.

A **CARCHARODONTOSAURUS** skull is about 1.5 metres (5 feet) long. That's about the average height of an adult human.

CRYOLOPHOSAURUS

PRONOUNCED: CRY-oh-LO-foh-SAWR-us

NAME MEANING: frozen-crested lizard

TIME PERIOD LIVED: Early Jurassic Period

LENGTH: 6 metres (20 feet)

WEIGHT: 363 kilograms (800 pounds)

TYPE OF EATER: carnivore

PHYSICAL FEATURES: sharp teeth; crest on top of its head

A **CRYOLOPHOSAURUS** skeleton was found with rib bones near its throat. At first scientists thought the dinosaur died choking on another animal's bones. Later scientists learned the ribs belonged to the Cryolophosaurus.

CRYOLOPHOSAURUS was one of the biggest meat-eating dinosaurs on Earth during the Early Jurassic Period.

CRYOLOPHOSAURUS' crest resembled a hairstyle worn by the famous singer Elvis Presley. Some scientists have nicknamed the dinosaur "Elvisaurus".

Cryolophosaurus lived in the forests of what is now Antarctica.

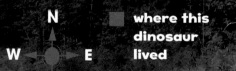

N
W • E
S

where this dinosaur lived

GASOSAURUS

PRONOUNCED: GAS-oh-SAWR-us

NAME MEANING: gas lizard

TIME PERIOD LIVED: Middle Jurassic Period

LENGTH: 3.7 metres (12 feet)

WEIGHT: 68 kilograms (150 pounds)

TYPE OF EATER: carnivore

PHYSICAL FEATURES: sharp teeth; big claws; strong back legs

GASOSAURUS used its arms to hold its prey while eating.

In 1972 a company drilling for gas found the only known GASOSAURUS fossils. This is how the dinosaur got its name.

Gasosaurus lived in the forests of what is now China.

N
W · E
S

☐ where this dinosaur lived

Some scientists believe the unearthed partial **GASOSAURUS** skeleton may have belonged to a young Gasosaurus. The dinosaur's skull has not been found.

GIGANOTOSAURUS

PRONOUNCED: gig-an-OH-toe-SAWR-us

NAME MEANING: giant southern reptile

TIME PERIOD LIVED: Late Cretaceous Period

LENGTH: 14 metres (45 feet)

WEIGHT: 8 metric tons (8.8 tons)

TYPE OF EATER: carnivore

PHYSICAL FEATURES: sharp teeth and claws; strong legs

GIGANOTOSAURUS' brain was about the size of a banana.

Giganotosaurus lived in the plains
and forests of what is now Argentina.

N
W E
S

where this
dinosaur lived

GIGANOTOSAURUS' teeth
were 20 centimetres (8 inches)
long and serrated like a knife.

Scientists think GIGANOTOSAURUS may have
been able to run up to 50 kilometres (31 miles)
per hour. That's faster than Tyrannosaurus rex.

NEOVENATOR

PRONOUNCED: KNEE-oh-veh-NAY-tur

NAME MEANING: new hunter

TIME PERIOD LIVED: Early Cretaceous Period

LENGTH: 7 metres (23 feet)

WEIGHT: 1 metric ton (1.1 tons)

TYPE OF EATER: carnivore

PHYSICAL FEATURES: small crests on its snout; strong neck; sharp claws and teeth

About 70 per cent of a complete **NEOVENATOR** skeleton has been found.

Neovenator lived in the swamps of what is now England.

N
W + E
S

■ where this dinosaur lived

NEOVENATOR had three clawed toes on each foot.

The first **NEOVENATOR** bones were found in 1978. They were seen sticking out of a cliff on the Isle of Wight in England.

OZRAPTOR

PRONOUNCED: oz-RAP-tur

NAME MEANING: thief of Oz; Oz is short for "Ozzies", a nickname for Australians

TIME PERIOD LIVED: Middle Jurassic Period

LENGTH: 2 metres (6.6 feet)

WEIGHT: 45 kilograms (100 pounds)

TYPE OF EATER: carnivore

PHYSICAL FEATURES: powerful jaws; sharp teeth; strong legs; stiff tail used for balance while running

In the mid-1960s, four boys found the first **OZRAPTOR** bone near Geraldton, Australia.

Ozraptor lived in the forests and plains of what is now Australia.

N
W E
S

where this dinosaur lived

OZRAPTOR was a hunter, but it was also a scavenger. It would eat dead animals.

OZRAPTOR is one of the oldest Australian dinosaurs.

SPINOSAURUS

PRONOUNCED: SPY-noh-SAWR-us

NAME MEANING: spine reptile

TIME PERIOD LIVED: middle Cretaceous Period

LENGTH: 16 metres (52.5 feet)

WEIGHT: 10 metric tons (11 tons)

TYPE OF EATER: carnivore

PHYSICAL FEATURES: sail down its back; long jaw; cone-shaped teeth; paddlelike feet for swimming

SPINOSAURUS spent most of its time in or near water. It splashed into the water looking for prey.

Spinosaurus lived near water in what are now Egypt and Morocco.

N
W — E
S

■ where this dinosaur lived

SPINOSAURUS had nostrils halfway up its snout. This helped it breathe while hunting in the water.

The original **SPINOSAURUS** specimen that was found in 1912 was destroyed during World War II (1939–1945).

SUCHOMIMUS

PRONOUNCED: SOO-cho-MYE-mus

NAME MEANING: crocodile mimic

TIME PERIOD LIVED: Late Cretaceous Period

LENGTH: 11 metres (36 feet)

WEIGHT: 4.4 metric tons (4.9 tons)

TYPE OF EATER: carnivore

PHYSICAL FEATURES: sail; long snout; sharp claws; strong arms

SUCHOMIMUS had nostrils that sat far up on its snout. This may have helped the dinosaur breathe while hunting in the water.

Suchomimus lived near lakes and rivers in what is now Niger.

N
W ← → E
S

■ where this dinosaur lived

SUCHOMIMUS had a 0.3-metre (1-foot) long thumb claw on each hand.

SUCHOMIMUS' teeth pointed backwards to grip slippery fish.

XUANHANOSAURUS

PRONOUNCED: shwan-HAN-oh-SAWR-us

NAME MEANING: Xuanhan County reptile; named after the site where it was found

TIME PERIOD LIVED: Middle Jurassic Period

LENGTH: 6 metres (19.7 feet)

WEIGHT: 227 kilograms (500 pounds)

TYPE OF EATER: carnivore

PHYSICAL FEATURES: sharp claws and teeth; strong arms and legs

XUANHANOSAURUS was discovered with a large number of other dinosaur fossils, including Gasosaurus.

Xuanhanosaurus lived in the forests of what is now China.

N
W • E
S

■ where this dinosaur lived

XUANHANOSAURUS is only known from a few bones, including a forelimb and shoulder bone.

XUANHANOSAURUS had three fingers on each hand.

GLOSSARY

CARNIVORE animal that eats only meat

CREST flat plate of bone

CRETACEOUS PERIOD third period of the Mesozoic Era; the Cretaceous Period was from 145 to 65 million years ago

FOSSIL remains of an animal or plant from millions of years ago that have turned to rock

JURASSIC PERIOD second period of the Mesozoic Era; the Jurassic Period was from 200 to 145 million years ago

NOSTRIL one of two openings in the nose used to breathe and smell

PLAIN large, flat area of land with few trees

PREY animal hunted by another animal for food

PRONOUNCE say a word in a certain way

QUARRY place where stone and other materials are dug from the ground

RELATIVE member of a family

SERRATED saw-toothed

SNOUT long front part of an animal's head; the snout includes the nose, mouth and jaws

SPECIMEN sample or an example used to stand for an entire group

WORLD WAR II war in which the United States, France, Great Britain, the Soviet Union and other countries defeated Germany, Italy and Japan; World War II lasted from 1939 to 1945

COMPREHENSION QUESTIONS

1. Scientists have found Allosaurus fossils at the Cleveland-Lloyd Quarry in Utah, USA. What is a quarry?

2. How did Gasosaurus get its name? Use the text to help you with your answer.

3. Suchomimus had nostrils far up on its snout. How did this help the dinosaur hunt for food?

READ MORE

Allosaurus and other Dinosaurs and Reptiles of the Upper Jurassic (Dinosaurs!), David West (Gareth Stevens Publishing, 2012)

Allosaurus vs. Brachiosaurus: Might Against Height (Dinosaur Wars), Michael O'Hearn (Raintree, 2011)

Dinosaurs in our Streets, David West (Franklin Watts, 2015)

WEBSITES

www.nhm.ac.uk/discover/dino-directory/index.html
At this Natural History Museum website you can learn more about dinosaurs through sorting them by name, country and even body shape!

www.show.me.uk/section/dinosaurs
This website has loads of fun things to do and see, including a dinosaur mask you can download and print, videos, games and Top Ten lists.

INDEX